ALL AROUND THE WORLD

UKRAINE

by Kristine Spanier, MLIS

pogo

Ideas for Parents and Teachers

Pogo Books let children practice reading informational text while introducing them to nonfiction features such as headings, labels, sidebars, maps, and diagrams, as well as a table of contents, glossary, and index.

Carefully leveled text with a strong photo match offers early fluent readers the support they need to succeed.

Before Reading

- "Walk" through the book and point out the various nonfiction features. Ask the student what purpose each feature serves.
- Look at the glossary together. Read and discuss the words.

Read the Book

- Have the child read the book independently.
- Invite him or her to list questions that arise from reading.

After Reading

- Discuss the child's questions. Talk about how he or she might find answers to those questions.
- Prompt the child to think more. Ask: Ukraine's national flower is the sunflower. Do you know what your country's national flower is?

Pogo Books are published by Jump!
5357 Penn Avenue South
Minneapolis, MN 55419
www.jumplibrary.com

Library of Congress Cataloging-in-Publication Data

Names: Spanier, Kristine, author.
Title: Ukraine / by Kristine Spanier, MLIS.
Description: Minneapolis, MN: Jump!, Inc., [2023]
Series: All around the world | Includes index.
Audience: Ages 7-10
Identifiers: LCCN 2022028452 (print)
LCCN 2022028453 (ebook)
ISBN 9798885242158 (hardcover)
ISBN 9798885242165 (paperback)
ISBN 9798885242172 (ebook)
Subjects: LCSH: Ukraine—Juvenile literature.
Classification: LCC DK508.515 .S63 2023 (print)
LCC DK508.515 (ebook)
DDC 947.7—dc23/eng/20220705
LC record available at https://lccn.loc.gov/2022028452
LC ebook record available at https://lccn.loc.gov/2022028453

Editor: Jenna Gleisner
Designer: Molly Ballanger

Photo Credits: Mahir Rustemov/Shutterstock, cover; Dobra Kobra/Shutterstock, 1; Pixfiction/Shutterstock, 3; Likman Uladzimir/Shutterstock, 4; Roman Mikhailiuk/Shutterstock, 5; JaySi/Shutterstock, 6-7; Vera Petrunina/Shutterstock, 8-9; SERGEI SUPINSKY/AFP/Getty, 10; Anatoly SAPRONENKOV/AFP/Getty, 11; Oleksandr GIMANOV/AFP/Getty, 12-13; Mny-Jhee/Shutterstock, 14; Bystrov/Shutterstock, 15 (borscht); knopka1228/Shutterstock, 15 (varenyky); Sergii Figurnyi/Shutterstock, 15 (holiday bread); Onix_Art/Shutterstock, 15 (background); A_Lesik/Shutterstock, 16-17; DmyTo/Shutterstock, 18-19; rospoint/Shutterstock, 20-21; Luts Iryna/Shutterstock, 23.

Printed in the United States of America at Corporate Graphics in North Mankato, Minnesota.

Information in this book reflects the status of Ukraine's government at the time of print.

TABLE OF CONTENTS

CHAPTER 1

SEA AND CITIES

Welcome to Ukraine! Do you like sunny beaches? There are many of them in Odesa! This city is on the coast. People enjoy swimming in the Black Sea.

Mount Hoverla

Ukraine is in eastern Europe. It is the second-largest country in Europe by land area. The Carpathian Mountains are in the southwest. Mount Hoverla is the highest point. It is 6,762 feet (2,061 meters) tall.

More than 40 million people live in Ukraine. Kyiv is the **capital**. Saint Sophia's Cathedral is here. It has 13 gold domes. The bell tower is 250 feet (76 m) high.

DID YOU KNOW?

The Dnieper River runs through Kyiv. It is Europe's fourth-longest river.

bell tower
Saint Sophia's Cathedral

Castle
Hill

Lviv is in the northwest. Lviv High Castle was built here in the 1360s. It was once the highest point in the city. Only pieces are left. Visitors can stand on Castle Hill and see wide views of this historic city.

WHAT DO YOU THINK?

Over time, people took pieces from Lviv High Castle to build other things. Do you think the castle should be rebuilt? Why or why not?

CHAPTER 2

FIGHT FOR FREEDOM

ballot

Ukrainians vote for a president. People also vote for members of the Verkhovna Rada. This group makes laws.

Ukraine was once part of the **Soviet Union**. Russia was the largest country in the Soviet Union. The Soviet Union broke apart in 1991. Ukraine gained **independence**. People gathered to celebrate.

Russia's military **invaded** Ukraine in February 2022. Why? Russia's leaders wanted more power. People of Ukraine **protested**. They fought back. A war started.

WHAT DO YOU THINK?

Lives are lost in war. People are hurt. Many leave their homes. Some leave the country. Do you think Ukrainians should be free to lead themselves? Why or why not?

protest

CHAPTER 3

DAILY LIFE

More than half of Ukraine is farmland. The country is one of the world's biggest grain producers. Ukraine also produces a lot of sunflower oil. The sunflower is Ukraine's national flower.

Borscht is the national dish. It is a beet soup. People also eat varenyky. These are potato dumplings. Bread is served at almost every meal. It is decorated for special occasions.

borscht

varenyky

holiday bread

кролик

Students study reading, writing, and math. They also have classes in art, nature, and music. In middle school, they can learn another language. German and English are two choices. After ninth grade, students choose if they want to continue high school.

For Easter, people paint designs on eggs. Independence Day is celebrated August 24. People watch fireworks and parades. Malanka is January 13. This is a celebration of the New Year.

TAKE A LOOK!

Decorated Easter eggs are called pysanky. Each color has a different meaning. Red is a **symbol** of hope. What do some of the designs on them mean? Take a look!

After a cold winter, some Ukrainians travel to the coast. Others hike the mountains to view waterfalls. Many enjoy celebrating their **heritage** at **folk** festivals.

There is much to know about Ukraine. What more would you like to learn?

QUICK FACTS & TOOLS

AT A GLANCE

UKRAINE

Location: eastern Europe

Size: 233,032 square miles (603,550 square kilometers)

Population: 43,528,136 (2022 estimate)

Capital: Kyiv

Type of Government: semi-presidential republic

Languages: Ukrainian (official), Russian

Exports: corn, sunflower oil, iron and iron products, wheat

Currency: hryvnia

GLOSSARY

capital: A city where government leaders meet.

eternity: All of time, without beginning or end.

folk: Traditional and belonging to the common people in a region.

heritage: Traditions and beliefs that a country or society considers an important part of its history.

independence: Freedom from a controlling authority.

invaded: Entered a place in order to occupy or control it.

protested: Demonstrated against something.

Soviet Union: A former country of 15 republics that included Russia, Ukraine, and other nations of eastern Europe and northern Asia.

symbol: An object or design that stands for, suggests, or represents something else.

Ukraine's currency

INDEX

TO LEARN MORE

Finding more information is as easy as 1, 2, 3.

1. Go to www.factsurfer.com
2. Enter "Ukraine" into the search box.
3. Choose your book to see a list of websites.